Ernest Roberts BA, PGCE, LCH, RSHom

Ernest Roberts was born in Lancashire and graduated in Economics from Manchester University in 1960. He worked as an economic forecaster and lectured in Management and Economics at the Thames Polytechnic. In 1977, Ernest began a career as a yoga teacher. He developed an original approach to therapy using all aspects of Yoga practice plus the twelve biochemic tissue salts, working with clients on a one to one basis. Yoga therapy produced many cures, but also led Ernest on to homœopathy. He attended Dr Thomas Maughan's classes and later was in the second intake at the College of Homœopathy in 1979.

In 1983 Ernest returned to Manchester and started in full time homœopathic practice. He founded the North West College of Homœopathy in 1984, of which he is Principal.

Dr Juliet Williams MB, BS, DSH

Juliet studied Medicine at Kings College Hospital, London and graduated in 1989. She then worked as a social researcher and policy analyst on health related issues with a particular interest in HIV and AIDS. Julie graduated from the School of Homœopathy in Devon in 1994. Her experience includes teaching and practising homœopathy in eastern Europe. She now practises in London. Julie teaches Human Sciences in a number of colleges of alternative medicine.

WARNING SIGNS
AND
SIMILAR SYMPTOMS

A Desktop Reference Guide for Alternative
and Complementary Practitioners

Ernest Roberts BA LCH RSHom
and
Juliet Williams MB BS DSH

Winter Press
29 Horniman Drive
London SE23 3BJ

First published by Winter Press in 1997

ISBN 1 874581 43 6

Cover design by Colin Winter

Printed by Biddles of Guildford, Surrey

This book is presented as a collection of signs and
symptoms and as an aid in diagnosis. It is
intended for use by professional practitioners and
not as a replacement for professional consultation
or treatment.

ACKNOWLEDGEMENTS

We would like to thank Dr David Curtin whose teaching inspired the idea of the need for this work and Dr Janina Iwaszko who contributed considerably to the early lectures at the North West College of Homœopathy. We would also like to acknowledge our colleague Constantine Petrondas RSHom who has always inspired a high standard of diagnostic skill in students and staff alike, and for assistance in proofreading and making invaluable suggestions to improve the text.

CONTENTS

FATIGUE - See Weakness

INTRODUCTION

This short work has grown out of regular lectures given to final year students and graduates of the North West College of Homœopathy in Manchester in order to revise and reinforce the knowledge required to recognize conditions which are dangerous and possibly life threatening; so as to facilitate prompt and accurate diagnosis and correct action required for the welfare and safety of patients.

The book describes:
1. Signs and symptoms of imminently dangerous or potentially dangerous conditions
2. Those conditions which have similar signs and symptoms to each other and might require urgent action
3. Differentiation of diagnostic signs and symptoms between urgent acute conditions and less urgent or potentially serious conditions.

Our aim is to enable the practitioner to identify situations where there is a risk of acute and serious deterioration in the patient's condition, and situations where the problem is mechanical in nature and hence calls for primarily surgical management. Conditions are also described where there is a serious chronic problem which requires accurate diagnosis and increased vigilance in case management.

The text is intentionally concise in style, so as to offer a quick desktop reference guide for practitioners, and therefore to supplement rather than to replace more detailed texts and teaching.

1.   *ABDOMINAL PAIN*

ACUTE ABDOMINAL PAIN

Serious conditions which can cause this are:

1.1   Inflammatory bowel disease, ie ulcerative colitis or Crohn's disease. Pain may be caused by an acute flare up of the chronic disorder, (accompanying symptoms are diarrhoea with blood and/or mucus in stools, loss of weight, loss of appetite, weakness and malaise).

1.2   Aortic aneurysm - pulsatile mass present, pain going through to back. Can rupture at any moment. Definitive treatment is with surgery to replace the blood vessel involved. In the meantime, homœopathic remedies can be used to relieve pain.

UPPER ABDOMINAL PAIN

1.3   Peptic ulceration (perforation or haemorrhage). Other symptoms include shock, pallor, rigidity of abdomen, vomiting of blood, black tarry stools (melaena); pain in the upper abdomen which can radiate through to the back.

1.4   Acute pancreatitis symptoms similar to above, apart from vomiting of blood being absent. Severe pain goes through to the back. It is most likely in those with a high consumption of alcohol, and can be diagnosed from tests of serum amylase level, but endoscopy may be performed to exclude peptic ulcer as the latter requires urgent surgery.

LOWER ABDOMINAL PAIN

1.5   Appendicitis begins with feeling vaguely unwell with slight fever, off food, nausea, perhaps vomiting and central abdominal pain. As the condition progresses, the pain becomes more severe and moves to the right iliac fossa, with rebound tenderness. The danger in this situation is that the appendix can become gangrenous and burst, leading to peritonitis.

1.6 Inflammation or stones affecting the ureter. (See also: Urinary System).

1.7 Ectopic pregnancy. The possibility of pregnancy should be enquired about in any woman of reproductive years who presents with abdominal or pelvic pain. If ectopic, there may not be missed periods. This is a serious condition, as the fallopian tube can rupture, leading to internal bleeding and peritonitis. A pregnancy test would be positive, and ultrasound scan would confirm the diagnosis. Surgery is required urgently.

1.8 Pelvic inflammatory disease can be severe and hence mimic acute appendicitis, though the pain may be either right or left sided. There can be fever and vaginal discharge. More common and more severe if an IUD (coil) is used. Conventional treatment is with antibiotics and pain relief.

1.9 Torsion or rupture of ovarian cyst. Torsion, although not life threatening produces severe pain, and usually an operation is performed forthwith. Rupture of a cyst produces pain rising to a crescendo which then subsides. There is no threat to life but without treatment the tendency to cysts may well be recurrent. An ultrasound scan will clarify diagnosis.

1.10 Endometriosis can cause severe abdominal or pelvic pain. There are likely to be modalities related to the menstrual cycle; ovulation is painful, menstruation is painful, sexual intercourse is painful, and conception can be difficult. The condition is a result of pieces of endometrial tissue being found in ectopic sites (outside the womb). They undergo all the same changes through the menstrual cycle as the lining of the womb, but there is no opportunity for the blood to be shed and this causes pain and the forrmation of cysts. Typically this occurs in the ovaries, fallopian tubes, pelvic cavity and sometimes more generally around the abdomen. Rarely it can affect the lungs and be a cause of haemoptysis.

1.11   Peritonitis. Any situation in which a part of the bowel can rupture can lead to peritonitis, which is an extremely serious condition characterised by rigid abdomen, pain, shock, pallor, low blood pressure and sweating. The patient needs to be admitted to hospital urgently.

1.12   Torsion of the testes. This condition should always be considered when a young male presents with lower abdominal pain. Although usually the testes is acutely swollen and painful, on some occasions severe abdominal pain may be the only symptom. The scrotum will however show signs of swelling and tenderness and should always be examined. Also enquire about trauma to the scrotum or previous attacks of pain of the testes. Torsion of the testes is an acute surgical emergency as if untreated the testes undergo irreversible infarction within a few hours.

2.   BACK PAIN

This is an extremely common complaint, and can come from many sources. Injuries and other known causes should be screened out. A physical examination by a suitably qualified professional is always advisable, and physical therapy such as osteopathy or spinal touch therapy should be considered.

2.1   Lower back pain. Once injury or mechanical damage has been screened out, the following should be considered:
Lower back pain can be referred from the reproductive organs. In women it could be due to dysmenorrhoea (painful periods), endometriosis, uterine prolapse (dragging pains), or more seriously from spread of cervical or uterine cancer to the spine. The latter is usually a disease of older women, at or beyond menopause; its chief symptom is abnormal bleeding - either between periods (InterMenstrual Bleeding - IMB) or after the menopause (Post Menopausal Bleeding - PMB).

Cervical cancer is classically described between the ages of 35 - 50, but is increasingly being diagnosed in women of a younger age. Symptoms of cervical cancer include abnormal vaginal discharge, with bad smell, or bleeding after sex (post coital bleeding); these symptoms are however not exclusive to cervical cancer. (See also: Vaginal Bleeding).

In men, cancer of the testes or of the prostate could spread to the spine. The symptoms of prostate cancer are identical to those of benign hypertrophy of the prostate, until the late stages of disease, ie frequency of urination, nocturia, dribbling, poor stream. Benign and malignant growths can be distinguished by a blood test. The state of the prostate can be determined by a rectal examination. These are advisable for male patients over the age of fifty. (See also: Urinary Tract - Prostate).

Malignant disease of the urinary tract should also be considered - painless haematuria is a classic sign of this. Tumours of the kidney can also lead to anaemia and to high blood pressure. (See also: Urinary Tract - Haematuria).

In summary, if a patient presents with low back pain of no obvious cause, careful enquiry should be made regarding sexual and urinary symptoms. Pain associated with malignancy will be of short, rapidly progressive history.

2.2   Shoulder pain. In women the possibility of breast cancer should be considered in the absence of obvious explanations. Pain can also be referred to the shoulder region from the gall bladder. (See also: Breast Problems, Gall Bladder).

2.3   Cancer - metastasis. Types of tumour which metastasise through the lymphatic system have a predilection to spread to bone, (and lungs, liver and brain); the most common of these are cancers of breast, lung, prostate, bladder and melanoma. Back pain of cancer in older people is nearly always from a cancer in an advanced stage.

2.4 Spinal cancer affects the gait and backache comes on with walking. The history of the pain is short and progressive. Primary tumours of bone can occur but are much rarer than secondary deposits of malignancy in bone (metastasis).

2.5 Children's pain in the loin. This could be from a kidney infection. Accompanying renal signs would give this diagnosis. It can develop as a complication of sore throat or tonsillitis and is a serious condition that you need to look out for.

2.6 Osteomyelitis (infection of the bone) can come on after a relatively minor injury or blow. As well as backache there is aching in the long bones of the legs, the patient is seriously ill with pains, fever and malaise.Urgent treatment is required; if neglected necrosis can occur and there is also a danger of septicaemia developing.

3. BREAST PROBLEMS

3.1 Breast cysts. Cysts of the breast are not uncommon, and are especially common around the time of menopause, as the breast tissue reacts to the changing hormones. Painful lumpy areas should be distinguished from a specific lump. If the lump is soft, rounded and mobile, it is more likely to be benign. A cancer usually feels hard, like bone, and may be attached either to the overlying skin or to deeper tissues such as the ribs and the chest wall.

Where the lump is unlikely to be malignant, reassurance is invaluable, because fear is a contributory factor in the formation of cancer. Give constitutional treatment and monitor the breasts regularly. Please remember to be gentle on examination. It is not uncommon for the vital force to form harmless cysts to act as deposits for toxins in harmless parts of the body like the breasts.

3.2   Breast cancer. Breast cancer is most common in women after the age of 50. The usual presenting symptom is a painless lump in the breast (see above). There may be the specific signs of puckering of the skin, peau d'orange (orange peel) skin, excema-like eruptions of the nipple, bloodstained discharge from the nipple. These are all signs of more advanced disease, and breast cancer can be present without any of these signs. The axilla should be examined for enlarged lymph nodes.

4.   *BREATHLESSNESS*

This is of serious concern if severe, worsening, unrelieved by usual medications, associated with pulse >120 and/or cyanosis. If the patient is too breathless to speak, they should be in hospital. If the bronchioles become totally constricted, the chest will sound silent rather than wheezy, and this again is an extremely serious situation.

5.   CANCER: GENERAL SIGNS AND SYMPTOMS

Malignant disease most commonly presents between the ages of 50 and 70, although there are some rare and generally aggressive tumours which occur in younger people.

General warning signs:
a)   Weight loss. TB and AIDS should also be considered.
b)   Fatigue. Causes of fatigue are numerous - both physical and otherwise.
c)   Malaise; loss of vitality, appetite and sexual drive. As above.
e)   Cracks in the skin, especially in the corners of the mouth.
f)   Yellow sclera of the eyes.
g)   Dark red, beefsteak tongue with cracks and fur.
h)   Sudden weakness of vision. (Could also be from Transient Ischaemic Attacks).
i)   A weak, discouraged pulse.
j)   Pearly tint to the eyes.

6.   CHEST PAIN

This can arise from:

6.1   Structures in the chest wall, eg tendonitis of pectorals, cracked rib. There may be an obvious history of trauma.

6.2   The breasts. For example acute or chronic mastitis, breast abscess.

6.3   Lower respiratory tract infection, ie lungs, bronchi, pleura, (would be accompanied by cough, shortness of breath, pain related to breathing and fever).

6.4   The oesophagus. Due to reflux of acid from the stomach producing 'heartburn'.

6.5   Cardiovascular system. Problems of the heart and great vessels, symptoms would include central stabbing or crushing pain; pain radiates to left arm and/or jaw; worse from exercise, cold, emotion, eating.

The situation is serious if cardiac pain continues beyond five minutes' duration and is unrelieved by usual medications or is more severe than usual. All these are warning signs of a heart attack being imminent. Immediate action is required; the indicated treatment should be given and urgent medical advice should be sought.

7.   *COUGH - PERSISTENT*

7.1   A smokers' cough tends to occur in the morning and to be clear and productive. If this is the case there is no immediate danger. Smoking affects the immune system, but not everyone is susceptible to lung cancer.

7.2   Non-productive dry coughs should clear up in two weeks; if not the possibilities of cancer, tuberculosis and pneumocystis carinii pneumonia (PCP) should be considered and investigated as appropriate, depending on the patient's age and background.

7.3   Drug effects; regular use of beta-blockers can produce a dry cough.

7.4   Cough can be a nervous (psychosomatic) symptom, but it is important that physical causes are excluded before this diagnosis is made.

7.5   Whooping cough can produce persistent cough without the characteristic whoop, especially in those who have been vaccinated, and this diagnosis is easily missed. Persistent cough in young children is regarded as indicative of asthma, even in the absence of the more characteristic wheezing.

8.   *DIABETES*

There are two forms of diabetes, Type 1 or juvenile onset and Type 2 or maturity onset. The former is more serious than the latter.

8.1   Juvenile Onset. In Type 1 diabetes, the body becomes unable to make its own insulin and insulin injections are needed to replace this. If previously undiagnosed, this is a serious situation in which urgent medical advice is needed. WITHOUT INSULIN THE PATIENT IS LIKELY TO DIE WITHIN A FEW DAYS.

The onset of this disease is typically between the ages of 8 and 14 years, and may follow an acute disease, eg urinary tract infection. Excessive thirst, excessive urination and weight loss despite seemingly adequate food intake are the typical symptoms, but one of these may be more predominant than the others. Lethargy and drowsiness after an acute disease should alert the practitioner to the possible onset of diabetes. Immediate hospital admission is appropriate to avoid this serious diagnosis being missed. There is often a hereditary factor.

If the diagnosis of diabetes has been established and the patient comes for alternative constitutional treatment, one might hope to see better control and stability of the condition, improved general health. Less susceptibility to long term complications can be achieved and acute situations can be treated successfully.

If there is a positive response to holistic treatment such as homœopathy, there may be an altered requirement for insulin and the regime needs to be reviewed. Many diabetics test either blood and/or urine glucose levels at home and are able to make adjustments accordingly. Obviously this is to be encouraged, but more frequent professional review may be needed.
INSULIN PRESCRIPTIONS MUST NEVER BE STOPPED – THE PATIENT CAN DIE OR GO INTO A COMA.

8.2   Maturity Onset. In an older person, Type 2 diabetes may be asymptomatic and detected by the presence of glucose in the urine at a routine health check. It is good practice with all patients over the age of fifty to test the urine, measure the blood pressure and take the pulse rate. Alternatively, there may be symptoms of fatigue, excessive thirst and excessive urination; or the patient may present with symptoms of diabetic complications. Type 2 diabetes can often be controlled through diet, but sometimes antihyperglycaemic drugs are also given. Insulin injections are seldom needed. However, there is no such thing as 'mild diabetes'. Even if the blood sugar is regulated satisfactorily with diet alone, there is still an increased risk of serious disease or death through complications involving the circulation, the eyes and the kidneys. Diabetics have increased susceptibility to infection and poor wound healing.

9.   DIZZY SPELLS

It is important to ascertain exactly what sensations are being experienced, eg light headedness or vertigo. In the latter case, determine the exact symptoms and use the repertory accordingly.

9.1   Light Headedness. Blood pressure should be taken; it may be low or fluctuating. Readings of 100/70 or 60 can be normal for some women, but this is not acceptable for men. If the patient takes antihypertensive drugs, the dose may be excessive. They should be referred to the prescriber of the medication for a review. The blood pressure could be reduced by internal haemorrhage - an extremely dangerous and urgent situation in which the patient should be transferred to hospital without delay. Other signs of this would be: rapid pulse rate, palpitations, sweating, pallor, tense abdomen.

9.2   Cardiac dysrhythmias can cause dizzy spells; the pulse may be irregular. If there is no obvious cause for the symptoms, or there is a history of heart disease, this possibility should be considered strongly. An ElectroCardioGram (ECG) should be taken, and evaluation by a cardiac specialist is needed.

9.3   Dehydration. This can occur in hot weather (ask what and how much the patient has drunk); in those on diuretics (ask about their medication, the elderly may take all their weekly medication at once for convenience!); in urinary tract disease (enquire about frequency, pain, haematuria, oedema); and in severe diarrhoea, be especially alert for this in children. The skin and tongue may appear dry, and the skin loses elasticity. If pinched, it is slow to return to normal.

9.4   Low blood sugar. If frequent, endocrine investigations should be made. If the patient is diabetic, their regime should be reviewed.

9.5   Arthritis of the cervical spine (cervical spondylosis) can cause dizziness or vertigo because the disordered bone leads to restriction of the blood vessels supplying the brain.

10.   EAR SYMPTOMS

These are most common in children under twelve years of age, the peak of incidence being between two and five years. The fever produced can lead to febrile convulsions in those who are susceptible and thus general advice is to sponge the child down from the centre outwards with cool or tepid water, and give the appropriate remedies.

10.1   Mastoiditis. This is indicated by pain and swelling behind the ear and worsening rather than resolution of existing symptoms. Mastoiditis most commonly develops after a middle ear infection. It is a life threatening condition as meningitis may ensue if it is not properly dealt with.

Diabetics need prompt treatment for any ear infection

as they do not heal well, and therefore there is an increased likelihood of spread of infection to the mastoid air cells.

11.   EYES

11.1   Injuries to the eye require specialist treatment and it is essential that you should know the location of your nearest Eye Hospital or Eye Emergency Clinic. The ambulance service should be called.

11.2   Painful red eye. Altered visual acuity is a far better guide to the seriousness or otherwise of the patient's condition than the extent of redness or the degree of discomfort.

11.3   Blindness or disturbed vision can occur in temporal arteritis. (See also: Headaches - Temporal Arteritis).

11.4   Detached retina. Should be considered if there is either sudden or gradual reduction of visual field or visual acuity. See 11.2.

12.   GALL BLADDER

12.1   Chronic gall bladder pain is usually due to stones. As in the kidney, stones predispose to infection, and infection predisposes to stones. Pain can be referred to the tip of the right shoulder blade. It is brought on , or aggravated by, fatty foods, which the patient will therefore tend to avoid, and accompanied by wind - either upwards or downwards. Gallstones can also produce post-hepatic jaundice.

12.2   Cholecystitis. Gallstones whilst uncomfortable are not dangerous, but can have acute exacerbations - cholecystitis. Here the pain becomes more constant and more severe, the patient is febrile and generally unwell. This condition should be differentiated from: peptic ulcer (better for eating), pancreatitis, appendicitis, right-sided pneumonia, and myocardial infarction.

Conventional treatment of gallstones can comprise:

> use of ultrasound to break up the stones
>
> endoscopic removal of the stones
>
> removal of the gall bladder through open surgery

The first two do nothing to prevent recurrence of gallstones, which is common.

12.3 The condition of gallstones needs to be differentiated from carcinoma of the head of the pancreas, (here jaundice is usually painless and the symptoms are vague until late in the course of the disease).

13. GASTROINTESTINAL HAEMORRHAGE

13.1 Vomiting of blood. This may be either fresh (red) blood or 'coffee ground' (dark coloured) vomit, where the blood has stayed in the stomach for long enough to be partly digested. Vomiting blood is indicative of bleeding in the upper part of the digestive tract. The most likely causes are complications of peptic ulcer, or bleeding from oesophageal varices - these latter are a complication of liver disease.

In either case, further bleeding is possible and could be massive and fatal. The patient should be admitted to hospital without delay. An ambulance should be called.

13.2 Rectal bleeding, again can be of fresh or dark blood. The latter comes from higher up the GI tract. The inflammatory bowel disorders, ulcerative colitis and Chrohn's disease, can produce diarhoea with blood and mucus, abdominal pain and distention. The most serious possibility is of carcinoma of the large intestine, suggested by recent change of bowel habit in combination with rectal bleeding. Diagnosis is made by sigmoidoscopy and barium enema.

14.   HAEMOPTYSIS

The discharge from haemoptysis is usually frothy, bright red blood that is coughed or hawked up from the lungs and spat out. This is found in the following conditions:

14.1   Tuberculosis. Other symptoms include weight loss and night sweats.

14.2   Mitral valve disease of the heart. There may well be a history of rheumatic fever. Cardiac murmurs and signs of heart failure should be sought on physical examination. Enquire about breathlessness, oedema and dizzy spells.

14.3   Lung cancer should be considered in any hoarseness or cough which persists more than three weeks without signs of infection, especially in smokers. Look for finger clubbing and lymph gland enlargement, and enquire about loss of weight or appetite.

15.   HAEMORRHAGE

Abnormal bleeding is always a serious sign - haemoptysis, haematemesis, haematuria, rectal bleeding, and vaginal bleeding other than during menses. (See also: Gastrointestinal Haemorrhage, Haemoptysis, Urinary Tract - Haematuria, Vaginal Bleeding).

16.   HEADACHES

These are one of the most common symptoms reported, but they can be an indication of serious problems in the following circumstances:

16.1   Raised intracranial pressure. This can be produced by either a tumour or haemorrhage inside the skull. Haemorrhage may result either from a recent head injury or from a congenital weakness. In either case, prompt surgical action can save life and prevent disability. Headaches of this type are worse in the morning on rising, of progressive severity and accompanied by neurological signs. This combination of symptoms requires urgent attention. The definitive investigation is by CT scan of the head and neck (which gives a more detailed image of internal organs than a plain X-ray).

16.2   Temporal arteritis. An inflammmation of the arteries due to autoimmune disease, which may be accompanied by polymyalgia rheumatica, and occurs in the elderly. Throbbing headache in the forehead area, with tenderness of the scalp. There is a risk of sudden blindness as the retinal artery can become involved. The ESR (erythrocyte sedimentation rate) would be raised, often greatly. Conventional treatment is with high dose steroids.

16.3   Meningitis. Should be suggested by the combination of fever, neck stiffness, photophobia and drowsiness. Straightening the legs aggravates pain in the head and neck, as the meninges are stretched. The disease can begin with vague symptoms resembling flu, and the danger is that a child can go from being vaguely unwell to being dead within the course of only a few hours. The appearance of a rash is a usual part of the course of the disease in the case of meningococcal meningitis (the most severe type), and therefore the appearance of skin symptoms should not be assumed to indicate improvement according to Hering's 'Law of Cure'.

16.4   High blood pressure. If symptoms such as throbbing or bursting headache or flushed face are present, this indicates that the blood pressure is severely raised.

16.5   More commmonly, headache is either caused by tension, leading to spasms in the muscles of the neck; migraine; or referred from extracranial sources such as earache, sinusitis, tooth problems, etc.

17.   *INTESTINAL OBSTRUCTION*

17.1   Complete constipation, (ie neither faeces nor flatus are passed) indicates intestinal obstruction. On examination of the abdomen bowel sounds may be either absent or increased and of high pitch. In the latter situation, visible peristalsis may be present in a thin person. Vomiting of faeces suggests that this situation is severe and/or has been neglected.

There may be mechanical obstruction which calls for surgical treatment - the patient should be admitted to hospital. Alternatively, there may be stasis of the intestine (also known as 'paralytic ileus').

17.2   Intussusception. 'Red currant jelly' stools, ie motions which contain mucus stained with blood, in an infant or young child indicate intussusception. Other symptoms include a sudden onset, with colic and pain, causing the child to draw his/her knees up, and possibly vomiting. This is a condition in which the bowel folds in upon itself, and can lead to damage through ischaemia, and ultimately to gangrenous necrosis of part of the intestine. Barium enema is used to confirm the diagnosis and the radiologist is sometimes able to correct the problem whilst conducting the investigation. Otherwise an operation is needed.

18. LUMPS

Enlarged lymph glands can be either :

18.1   Localised (eg in groin, in neck, in axilla), which can arise from localised infection (eg of ear, with swollen glands in neck); secondary carcinoma; primary malignancy (lymphoma).

or

18.2   Generalised, which can be due to: generalised infection (eg glandular fever, TB, HIV) or to advanced stages of lymphoma or leukaemia.

The lymph drainage of organs which are common sites of tumours, eg breast, stomach should be learnt. For example, enlargement of Virschoff's lymph node (above the mid-clavicular point on the left side) is a sign of stomach cancer.

18.3   If the patient has a lump in their neck, the thyroid gland should be examined; this is done from behind. A lump associated with the thyroid will rise and fall on swallowing - you can watch the patient drink a glass of water. Sometimes there are no symptoms other than the enlargment - the hormone levels may be normal. Otherwise there will be the usual symptoms of hyper- or hypo-thyroidism. The pulse and blood pressure should be checked in thyroid disease.

See also: Section 23. Skin Growths.

19. NASAL OBSTRUCTION

Small children often push something up their nose which then gets stuck. If this goes unnoticed a one-sided offensive discharge may develop. They should be taken to the ENT clinic (via Casualty) to have the foreign body removed.

20. PALLOR

This is a characteristic sign of anaemia. The colour or otherwise of the conjunctiva is a more reliable guide than the colour of the skin. There are various types and causes of anaemia; they are distinguished by causation, and identified in the laboratory by the results of a full blood count, in which the size as well as the numbers of the various blood cell types is measured.

Older people may present simply with stomach pain, loss of appetite and weakness without any of the other classic symptoms of anaemia being present. Investigations are necessary for the correct diagnosis to be reached, and to exclude other possibilities.

20.1   Iron deficiency anaemia. Blood cells are small (microcytic).
This can be due to lack of iron in the diet, or to excess blood loss, or the increased demands of pregnancy. Sources of bleeding should be enquired into - recent injury, heavy periods, etc. Anaemia can be produced by bleeding into the bowel, and hence can be the first sign of cancer of the large intestine. This should be borne in mind, especially if the patient is over 50, has lost weight recently, has had ulcerative colitis, or has a family history of rectal cancer.

20.2   Anaemia accompanying chronic disease, eg rheumatoid arthritis, kidney disease. Normocytic - the red blood cells are of normal size.

20.3   Haemolytic anaemias, eg sickle cell. These occur when the blood cells are abnormal and hence are destroyed at a higher rate of turnover than normal. This can also give rise to pre-hepatic jaundice. They are detected by haemoglobin electrophoresis.

20.4   Aplastic anaemia. This means the impaired production of cells, due to damage or malfunction of the bone marrow. There are reduced numbers of red cells, but they are of a normal size. The bone marrow may be damaged by the effects of drugs, eg gold, penicillamine, cytotoxics, AZT, or this could be a sign of leukaemia. The blood count should be supplemented by a blood film (for microscopic examination) to check this possibility if there is no other obvious explanation.

20.5   Folate deficiency anaemia. Large cells (macrocytic). Most common during pregnancy. Usually remedied by increasing dietary intake and supplements. Some drugs can impair absorption of folate in the diet, particularly anticonvulsants.

20.6   Pernicious anaemia - deficiency of Vitamin B12. Large cells (macrocytic). Can be due to dietary deficiency (vegans), malabsorption (disease or removal of stomach) or autoimmune disease. The skin has a lemon-yellow tinge, the hair snow white, and mild jaundice may be present. The tongue may be tender, smooth and red. The condition can develop to include peripheral neuropathy (this may be the presenting symptom) and sub-acute combined degeneration of the spinal cord.

21.   PALPITATIONS

This can be serious if frequently occuring, rapid or accompanied by: chest pain, dizziness or fainting. The nature and cause of palpitations can be determined from analysis of an ECG.

21.1   Palpitations are common in states of hormone disturbance, hence around the time of the menopause.

21.2   Thyroid disease should also be considered - ask about characteristic symptoms, eg temperature modalities; take pulse and blood pressure. Hyperthyroidism can weaken the heart in the long term if untreated. Such patients should have regular monitoring of their condition.

22.   REFLEXES - ABNORMAL

Increased (brisk) reflexes are found in upper motor neuron disorders; sluggish reflexes in lower motor neuron disorders. A specific, localised impairment suggests the possibility of tumour of the brain or spinal cord; syringomyelia (a disease in which cysts develop on the spinal cord - extremely rare); or could be the results of a stroke or of multiple sclerosis. Disturbance of several reflexes suggests a systemic neurological disorder.

22.1.   Multiple sclerosis tends to follow an episodic course of remittance and relapse. It can be hard to diagnose in the early stages, and therefore may not be identified until a relatively late stage. In such neurological conditions the possible symptoms are very diverse. Visual disturbance, double vision, tingling or pins and needles and weakness of any of the limbs are common early symptoms of multiple sclerosis.

23.   SKIN GROWTHS

Remember that less aggressive forms of skin cancer can be a kind of safety valve, and with older people or those with a history of more serious internal pathology it could be dangerous to suppress them. However a rodent ulcer which does not respond to treatment may need to be excised.

23.1   The most serious type of skin cancer is malignant melanoma. This can arise de novo or through malignant change in an existing mole. Characteristics are: increasing size, irregular edge, irregular colouration, itching, bleeding. The patient can use tracing paper to trace the outline of the lesion to see if its size and shape change over time; this should be done monthly. If growth is observed, prompt action should be taken, as the main risk of melanoma is its aggressive growth and ready propensity for distant spread.

23.2   Basal cell carcinoma (rodent ulcer). This often appears
        in a butterfly or triangular shape on the cheek or bridge
        of the nose, with a slightly pearly appearance and an
        irregular outline. It can alternatively take the form of a
        central ulcer surrounded by a raised pearly edge. Small
        blood vessels spread out from the side of the lesion.
        Conventionally, these are not regarded as a particularly
        aggressive type of tumour, and seldom metastasise.
        Treatment is by either surgical excision or radiotherapy,
        depending on which is more practical in the site
        involved.

23.3   Squamous cell carcinoma. These can either form an out-
        growth a little like a wart or be flat and eating into the
        skin. They can become infected. These tend to be found
        on exposed parts of the skin, on individuals who have
        worked outside or otherwise been exposed to the ele-
        ments.

24.   SWALLOWING

24.1   Thyroid swellings can cause pressure symptoms in the
        throat. Enquire after thyroid-related symptoms (reac-
        tion to heat and cold, appetite and weight, functioning
        of bowels and of menstrual cycle, mental functioning);
        examine the throat for swellings; take pulse and blood
        pressure readings; arrange blood tests for levels of thy-
        roid hormones.

24.2   Cancer of the oesophagus should be considered, espe-
        cially in smokers and spirit drinkers. Look for enlarged
        lymph nodes in the neck; short and rapid progression
        of disease. Barium swallow will demonstrate mechani-
        cal constriction of the throat and/or oesophagus.

24.3   Motor neurone disease makes co-ordination of the
        oesophagus difficult; this is known as 'achalasia'. The
        nerves are affected by the pathology and hence the
        muscles do not function correctly, with the result that

the oesophagus bulges out like a second stomach. This is quite rare.

24.4   Persistent lump or sensation of lump in the throat may be 'globus hystericus'. If emotions are not expressed, look at the case history. This condition is most often found in sensitive middle-aged women.

25.   URINARY TRACT

25.1   Prostatic hypertrophy. This is common in men of middle age and older, in whom the prostate gland is commonly enlarged. This means that the urethra is constricted and hence the flow of urine is impaired, and it becomes difficult for the bladder to empty completely. The signs of benign prostatic hypertrophy are:
> Poor stream of urine.
> Slow start to urination.
> Dribbling at the end.
> Getting up several times at night to empty the bladder.

Although this is common (affects 65% of men over 85) and a benign condition, if the bladder does not empty properly, this predisposes to urinary infections, and if the condition becomes severe there can be complete retention of urine.

25.2   Tumours of the prostate. Enlargement of the prostate due to benign hypertrophy and due to a malignant tumour will produce the same symptoms. These can be distinguished by the combination of a blood test and rectal examination.

25.3   Cystitis. Infection of the lower urinary tract is common in women, but rare in men, where it could indicate the presence of a more serious underlying disorder, eg diabetes, or be a complication of prostatic enlargement (see above). In children, recurrent urinary infections could be due to structural anomalies of the kidneys or urinary tract, (these would be shown on an Intra Venous

Pyelogram - IVP), or the possibility of sexual abuse should be considered (vaginal bleeding before puberty is also to be taken seriously for the same reason).

In women who experience cystitis, bacteria cannot always be cultured form the urine, but despite this it is common for antibiotics to be prescribed. Conversely, there can be bacteria present but no symptoms.

In pregnant women, there is an increased likelihood of infection spreading upwards to the kidneys, (ie a deeper and more vital level of the body) to cause pyelonephritis. The development of loin pains with fever, chills and perhaps vomiting would indicate this.

25.4   Kidney stones. This produces one sided, sharp pain in the loin: 'renal colic'. If the stone leaves the kidney for the ureter, the pain will follow its line. The pain is excrutiating and the patient writhes around, unable to keep still, they are slightly ameliorated by doubling up. Conventional treatment is with pain relief and antibiotics. Complications are rare unless there is a structural abnormality or underlying chronic disease such as diabetes. Fever which is very high, prolonged or relapsing and worsening symptoms indicate deterioration.

25.5   Retention of urine. No urine being passed, or only a little (less than a pint a day), is a medically urgent situation which calls for immediate action. If stones are causing an obstruction, these may be broken up with ultrasound or else removed surgically.

HAEMATURIA

25.6   Blood in the urine may be present if there is a severe infection of the urinary tract and this will be accompanied by pain, frequency, urging and perhaps fever.

25.7   Painless haematuria is a classic sign of cancer of the kidneys or bladder, and should be regarded as such until proven otherwise.

25.8   Blood abnormalities. In any abnormal bleeding the symptoms may be due to an abnormality of the blood, (eg a clotting problem, excessive anticoagulation, or leukaemia) or a disease of the part from which the blood comes.

26. VAGINAL BLEEDING

This is serious in the following circumstances:

26.1   Before puberty. This could indicate sexual abuse.

26.2   After the menopause. This is a classic sign of carcinoma of the endometrium, unless the woman is on HRT - when a 'menstrual cycle' continues artificially - and so this symptom is more difficult to diagnose accurately.

26.3   During pregnancy. In early pregnancy the most likely explanation is threatened or inevitable miscarriage. In later pregnancy, placenta praevia or placental abruption are possible and there is a risk of further and torrential haemorrhage. Urgent advice should be sought from the midwife or the GP, and the patient should not be moved.

26.4   In between menstrual periods. Another classic sign of carcinoma of the endometrium, most likely after the age of forty.

26.5   After sexual intercourse. This could indicate carcinoma of the cervix.

27.   VOICE - CHANGE OF

27.1   A dull monotonous voice lacking emotion demonstrates great weakness and would often indicate serious pathology.

27.2   Any hoarseness which has persisted over three weeks in the absence of infection could indicate cancer of the throat or larynx, especially in smokers. Patients with this symptom should be advised to return for regular consultations. If constitutional treatment does not clear the throat symptoms completely, then cancer should be suspected and the case treated accordingly.

27.3   A low voice can come from HYPOTHYROIDISM. Look for changes in the skin and hair, slow pulse, slow thinking and constipation. If untreated serious mental symptoms and eventually coma can ensue.

28.   WEAKNESS

Fatigue is one of the most common symptoms presented. There can be either a physical (organic) or emotional cause. Being a very general symptom, it lacks specificity and hence is not very helpful in either diagnosis or remedy selection. Careful enquiry should be made during the case taking to cover the wide range of possibilities, including medications. If there is no obvious cause the following tests may be helpful:
   a) Full blood count
   b) Electrolyte levels
   c) Liver function
   d) Kidney function
   e) Thyroid hormone levels
   f) Testing the urine for glucose

28.1   Endocrine disturbance should be considered. Hypothyroidism is most common at the menopause or following childbirth. Lack of steroid hormones, though much rarer, could also give this symptom - enquire about steroid prescriptions. Diabetes should also be considered - enquire about appetite, weight, diet, urination and family history.

28.2   In the elderly, weakness could be a general symptom of cancer or anaemia.

28.3   In younger people, pancreatic disease, malabsorption, chronic infection and HIV should be considered.

28.4   If TB is suspected a chest X-ray will usually confirm or refute the diagnosis.

29.   WEIGHT LOSS

Weight loss should be regarded as a serious cause of concern if it is severe, progressive, unexplained or accompanied by mental symptoms of distorted body image.

29.1   Cancer. A loss of 2kg (5lb) in a month for no apparant reason is suspicious, particularly if the patient is over 45. In older people this could be indicative of cancer. The totality of symptoms should be assessed with this in mind.

29.2   Malabsorption. In a younger person, there could be disorder of the pancreas or some other form of malabsorption, including that due to inflammatory bowel disease. Hyperthyroidism can lead to weight loss despite a good or increased appetite.

29.3   Diabetes. In a child or adolescent, the onset of Type 1 diabetes should be considered, and a urine test for glucose would be appropriate. One would also expect to find symptoms of fatigue and profuse urination. Diabetes can appear after an acute infectious disease, eg urinary infection. (See also: Diabetes).

29.4   TB. If the patient has travelled abroad or lived in deprived conditions, consider tuberculosis. Lymph nodes are likey to be enlarged. Enquire about night sweats and cough.

29.5   HIV. HIV disease could be another possible cause of unexplained weight loss. Night sweats and persistent generalised lymphodenopathy (swollen lymph glands) may also be present. History of, and symptoms of, infections - which can include a very wide variety of conditions - should be enquired into.

29.6   Anorexia Nervosa. Extreme weight loss can be seen in some cases of this eating disorder when there are accompanying mental symptoms of distorted body image and a preoccupation with weight, appearance and diet. The menses often cease and there may be psychological issues concerning sexuality and the process of maturation. Induced vomiting or purging, in addition to reduced food intake, can lead to physical symptoms involving the gastro-intestinal tract. The mental symptoms reflect a deep and chronic level of disturbance for which a variety of support is advisable, including psychological approaches as well as specific treatment.

BIBLIOGRAPHY

1. E M Roberts, "What's in a Name", The Homœopath, Autumn 1996.
2. Sylvia Walker, "Spinal Touch Therapy", Spinal Touch Association.
3. Stephen Gascoigne, "The Manual of Conventional Medicine for Alternative Practitioners", Jigme Press.
4. Stephen Gascoigne, "Prescribed Drugs and the Alternative Practitioner", Ashgrove Press.
5. Peter Parish, "Medicines", Penguin Books.
6. "British National Formulary", HMSO Publications, published biannually.
7. R Robinson and R Stott, "Medical Emergencies - Diagnosis and Management".
8. D Rubenstein and D Wayne, "Lecture Notes on General Medicine", Blackwell Publications.
9. D Ellis and R Calne, "Lecture Notes on General Surgery", Blackwell Publications.
10. "ABC of Ophthalmology", BMJ Publications.
11. M Adler (ed), "ABC of AIDS", BMJ Publications.
12. PD Bull, "Lecture Notes on Diseases of the Ear, Nose and Throat", Blackwell Publications.
13. Kumar and Clarke, "Clinical Medicine".
14. Souhami and Moxham, "A Textbook of Medicine".
15. N Rowley, "Hands On", Hodder and Stoughton.
16. M Tyler, "Homœopathic Drug Pictures", B Jain.
17. "What the Doctors Don't Tell You Guide to Medical Tests", Wallace Press.
18. "What the Doctors Don't Tell You Guide to the Side Effects of Drugs", Wallace Press.
19. Thomas Kreuzel ND, "The Homœopathic Emergency Guide", North Atlantic Books: Berkely, California.
20. B. Day, "Select Your Remedy", Jain: Bombay.
21. D. Borland, "Homœopathy in Practice", Beaconsfield.

SIGNS & SYMPTOMS OF SOME ACUTE AND URGENT CONDITIONS

✔ possible symptoms
𝓦 key symptoms

Condition	Abnormal behaviour	Abnormal discharge	Blueness	Breathing difficulty	Breathing noisy	Cough	Deformity / Swelling	Diarrhoea	Fever	Headache	Itching	Loss of function	Pain	Rash	Tenderness	Unconsciousness	Vomiting
Appendicitis								✔	𝓦				𝓦		𝓦		✔
Asthma			✔	𝓦	𝓦	𝓦											✔
Bronchitis				✔	✔	𝓦			𝓦				✔				
Chicken pox									𝓦	✔	𝓦			𝓦			
Cholecystitis									✔				𝓦				✔
Common cold		✔				✔			𝓦	✔							
Concussion	𝓦		✔							𝓦		✔				𝓦	✔
Convulsions	✔		✔	𝓦	𝓦				✔							𝓦	✔
Convulsions febrile	𝓦		𝓦	✔					𝓦							𝓦	
Croup			✔	𝓦	𝓦	𝓦			𝓦				✔				✔
Cystitis									✔				𝓦		✔		✔
Dysentery								𝓦	𝓦				𝓦		✔		✔
Earache									✔	✔			𝓦		𝓦		✔
Ectopic pregnancy		✔											𝓦		𝓦		
Encephalitis	𝓦								𝓦	𝓦						✔	𝓦
Food poisoning								𝓦	✔	✔			𝓦				𝓦
Fracture							𝓦					𝓦	𝓦		✔		
Gastroenteritis								𝓦	𝓦				𝓦		✔		𝓦
Glandular fever							✔		𝓦	✔			𝓦	✔			
Hay fever		𝓦				✔				✔	𝓦						
Heart attack		✔	✔						✔				𝓦			✔	✔
Heart failure		✔	𝓦	✔									✔			✔	✔
Hepatitis								𝓦	✔	✔			✔				✔
Influenza						𝓦		✔	𝓦	✔			𝓦				✔

40

	Abnormal behaviour	Abnormal discharge	Blueness	Breathing difficulty	Breathing noisy	Cough	Deformity / Swelling	Diarrhœa	Fever	Headache	Itching	Loss of function	Pain	Rash	Tenderness	Unconciousness	Vomiting
Intususseption	✔	✔										✔	✔		✔		✔
Kidney stones		✔							✔			✔	✔				
Leukaemia									✔			✔	✔				
Mastoiditis	✔						✔		✔	✔		✔			✔		✔
Measles						✔			✔	✔	✔			✔			✔
Meningitis	✔								✔	✔				✔		✔	✔
Mumps							✔		✔	✔		✔			✔		✔
Nephritis									✔	✔						✔	✔
Osteomyelitis									✔	✔		✔	✔		✔	✔	✔
P.I.D.	✔								✔			✔	✔				
Peptic ulceration	✔							✔					✔		✔		✔
Pneumonia			✔	✔	✔	✔			✔	✔		✔					✔
Poisoning	✔			✔	✔	✔	✔	✔	✔				✔			✔	✔
Polio				✔					✔	✔		✔	✔				✔
Rubella									✔					✔			
Septicaemia		✔							✔	✔						✔	✔
Sinusitis		✔					✔		✔	✔		✔	✔				
Sore throat						✔	✔		✔	✔		✔	✔	✔			✔
Stroke	✔			✔								✔					✔
Tetanus				✔	✔				✔	✔		✔	✔		✔		
Tonsillitis				✔	✔	✔			✔	✔		✔	✔	✔			✔
Viruses				✔	✔	✔		✔	✔	✔		✔	✔				✔
Whooping cough			✔	✔	✔	✔			✔								✔

NOTIFIABLE INFECTIOUS DISEASES

There are a number of infectious diseases which it is required that the practitioner treating anyone with the disease informs their local health authority. The following is a sample list although the diseases may vary slightly from one local authority to another and also from time to time. It is advisable that all practitioners write to their local health authority and request a list of their Statutory Notifiable Infectious Diseases.

Acute encephalitis	Ophthalmia neonatorum
Acute meningitis	Paratyphoid fever
Acute poliomyelitis	Plague
Anthrax	Rabies
Cholera	Relapsing fever
Diphtheria	Scarlet fever
Dysentery	Smallpox
Food poisoning	Tetanus
Infective jaundice	Tuberculosis
Lassa fever	Typhoid fever
Leprosy	Typhus fever
Leptospirosis	Viral haemorrhagic fever
Malaria	Whooping cough
Marburg disease	Yellow fever
Measles	

DISEASES IT IS ILLEGAL TO TREAT

The Medicines Act 1968 forbids recommendation other than by a Medical Doctor in respect of the following conditions:

Tuberculosis
Cancer
Diabetes
Epilepsy or fits
Paralysis
Cataract
Glaucoma
Locomotor Ataxia
Sexually transmitted diseases
AIDS
Kidney Disease (including Bright's disease)

INDEX

This index gives references not found in the contents pages.